THE BIG THREE
ZEUS, POSEIDON AND HADES

Mythology 4th Grade

Children's Greek & Roman Books

BABY PROFESSOR

EDUCATION KIDS

Speedy Publishing LLC

40 E. Main St. #1156

Newark, DE 19711

www.speedypublishing.com

Copyright 2017

The Greeks had many gods and many myths and stories surrounding them. Greek mythology tells the tales about the many Greek gods, goddesses and heroes. In this book, we will be learning about Zeus, Poseidon and Hades.

ZEUS

Zeus lived on Mount Olympus, was married to a goddess by the name of Hera, and was king of the Greek gods. He was god of lightning, thunder, and the sky and his symbols included the eagle, the oak tree, the lightning bolt and the bull.

Zeus

HIS POWERS

Zeus held the most power of the Greek gods, having many powers. His most notable power was his ability to throw bolts of lightning. Pegasus, his winged horse, carried these lightning bolts and he had trained an eagle to return them. He also had the ability to control weather causing rain along with tremendous storms.

He also had some other powers and could mimic a person's voice to sound like anyone. Additionally, he could shape shift which made him look like a person or an animal. If someone angered him, he would then turn them into an animal for punishment.

HIS BROTHERS AND SISTERS

Zeus had many sisters and brothers who were also powerful goddesses and gods. Even though Zeus was the youngest, he was the most powerful of his three brothers. Hades, his older brother, ruled the Underworld. Poseidon, his other brother, was God of the seas. Zeus also had three sisters that included Hestia, Demeter and Hera, the latter of whom he married.

CHILDREN

Zeus had several children, some of which were Olympic gods, Apollo, Aries, Athena, Artemis, Aphrodite Hermes, Aphrodite and Dionysus. He also was father to some that were half-human and some were heroes including Hercules and Perseus. His other children that were famous included the Graces, the Muses and Helen of Troy.

Perseus on Pegasus

Rhea and Cronus

BECOMING KING OF THE GODS

Zeus was born the sixth child of the Titan gods Rhea and Cronus. His father Cronus worried that his children might become too powerful so he ate the first five children born. However, they did not die, but they also could not get out of his stomach! When Zeus was born, she hid him from his father Cronus. Zeus was then raised by Nymphs in the forest.

As he grew older Zeus wanted to rescue his sisters and brothers. He was able to obtain a special potion and disguised himself so that his father would not be able to recognize him. As Cronus drank it, he coughed up the five children. These five children were Hestia, Hades, Poseidon, Hera and Demeter.

Chronos

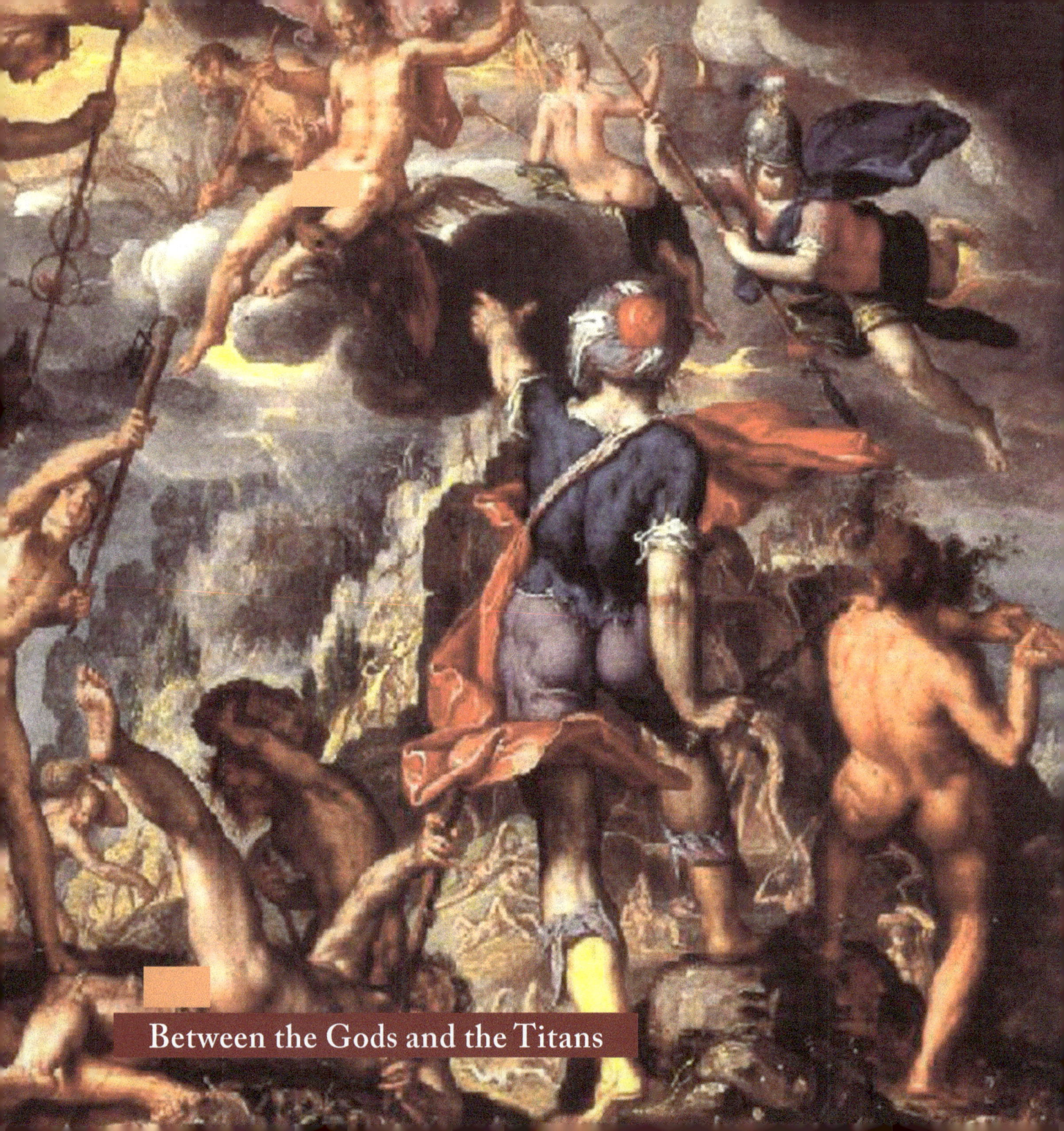

Between the Gods and the Titans

This angered Cronus as well as the Titans. They fought Zeus as well as his sisters and brothers for several years. Zeus then freed the Giants and the Cyclops of Earth to assist in this fight. They provided the Olympians with weapons for fighting the Titans. Zeus received lightning and thunder, Poseidon received a powerful trident, and Hades received a helm, making him invisible. The Titans proceeded to surrender and Zeus had them locked up deep in the underground.

Soon, Mother Earth became angry about Zeus locking up the Titans underground and she sent the Typhoon, the most fearsome of the world, to fight the Olympians. Zeus did not hide, even though the other Olympians did. He fought with the Typhoon and was able to trap him underneath Mount Etna, which is where the legend of Mount Etna becoming a volcano started.

Mount Etna

Mount Olympus

Zeus was now the most powerful of all gods. Along with his fellow gods, he moved to Mount Olympus. It was there that he ruled over the humans and gods and married Hera.

POSEIDON

Poseidon is one of the 12 Olympians and is a Greek mythology god. He is known to be one of the three most powerful gods, along with Hades and Zeus, and rules over all bodies of water, including the ocean. He was particularly important to fishermen and Greek sailors.

HOW WAS POSEIDON TYPICALLY PICTURED?

Typically, he is pictured with a trident, a three pronged spear. His hair is usually curly and he typically has a beard. Occasionally he might be shown riding his chariots pulled by hippocampuses, which are horses that have fish tails.

WHAT WERE HIS SKILLS AND POWERS?

He had total power and control over the ocean and was able to create storms that would sink ships or clear weather for helping them along. He was also able to cause earthquakes which earned him the name "earth-shaker".

BIRTH OF POSEIDON

He was the son Rhea and Cronus, who were the king and queen of the Titans. After Poseidon was born, his father Cronus swallowed him because of a prophecy that said Cronus's children someday would overtake him. Eventually, Poseidon was saved by Zeus, his younger brother.

DEFEAT OF THE TITANS

Along with his brothers, Hades and Zeus, they proceeded to battle the Titans and were able to overthrow them and take control over the world. They decided to divide the world by picking lots. Poseidon drew the ocean, taking control of the Sea. Hades, the Underworld and Zeus, the sky.

CREATION OF THE HORSE

Creating the horse was one of Poseidon's most infamous deeds. There are two different stories telling how this was accomplished. The first one states that he fell in love with the goddess Demeter, and to impress her he decided to make the most beautiful animal in the world. He worked for quite some time and was able to eventually produce the horse. It took him so long, however, to make it that he decided he was no longer in love with her. The second-story states that he made the horse to win the city of Athens from Athena.

RIVALRY WITH ATHENA

Athena and Poseidon both desired to be patron god of Athens. Part of the contest was giving a gift to Athens leaders. Athena created an olive tree to help with producing olives, olive oil and wood. Poseidon presented them with the horse, which would be valuable in battle, transportation and work. It was noted in some stories that instead of the horse, he presented them with a well of sea water.

Athena

Athena Statue

It was Athena who won this contest and would become patron goddess of Athens. Athena and Poseidon became rivals from that time on, which played out in the story of the Odyssey where Poseidon attempted to impede Odysseus, while Athena tried to help him with his journey.

HADES

Hades is a Greek mythology god that rules over the Underworld and, along with his brothers Poseidon and Zeus, is known to be one of the three most commanding Greek gods.

HOW WAS HADES TYPICALLY PICTURED?

He typically had a beard, a crown or helmet, while holding a pitchfork or a staff. He would often have Cerberus, his three-headed dog, with him. While traveling, he rides in a chariot that is pulled using black horses.

WHAT SKILLS AND POWERS DID HADES HAVE?

He had total control over the Underworld as well as all of its subjects. In addition to being an immortal god, invisibility was one of his powers. He wore the Helm of Darkness, which was a helmet that provided him with invisibility. He loaned it once to Perseus to help him defeat Medusa.

Perseus

Hades

BIRTH OF HADES

Hades was born to Rhea and Cronus, who were the queen and king of the Titans. After he was born, his father Cronus swallowed him to prevent the prophecy that his son would overthrow him one day. Eventually, Hades was saved by Zeus, his younger brother. Once the Olympians had defeated the Titans, along with his brothers, Hades decided to draw lots for division of the world.

Hades acquired the Underworld, Poseidon acquired the sea, and Zeus acquired the sky. The Underworld is known as where dead people go to in Greek mythology. At first, he was not happy with his draw, but once it was explained by Zeus that eventually all people would be his subjects, he was good with it.

Hades and his pet Cerberus

Hades had a huge three-headed dog which went by the name of Cerberus to protect his realm and he guarded the Underworld entrance. He was there to keep the dead from escaping and the living from entering.

CHARON

Charon was another one of Hades' helpers and was his ferryman. He would put the dead on a boat and take them across the rivers Acheron and Styx from the living world to the Underworld. The dead even had to pay Charon to cross or they had to wander the shores for a hundred years.

Hades abducts Persephone

PERSEPHONE

Hades had become quite lonely and wanted a wife. Zeus told him that he could marry Persephone, his daughter. Persephone, however, did not want to marry him and reside in the Underworld. Hades proceeded to kidnap her and forced her to the Underworld.

Persephone's mother, Demeter, who was also the goddess of crops, became depressed and neglected her harvest causing world famine. The gods eventually came to agreement and Persephone would only live with Hades four months out of the year. The months were represented by winter, when no harvest would grow.

Demeter

These are only three of the many gods surrounding Greek mythology and there is so much more to learn. There are so many legends, myths, heroes, and gods to learn about.

For additional information, you can go to your local library, research the internet, and ask questions of your teachers, family and friends.

Milton Keynes UK
Ingram Content Group UK Ltd.
UKHW050450050924
447908UK00003B/5

9 798869 413680